A KEY TO

TENNYSON'S 'IN MEMORIAM,'

BY

ALFRED GATTY, D.D.,

Vicar of Ecclesfield and Sub-Dean of York.

LONDON:

DAVID BOGUE,

3, St. Martin's Place, Trafalgar Square.

1881.

HASKELL HOUSE PUBLISHERS Ltd.

Publishers of Scarce Scholarly Books

NEW YORK. N. Y. 10012

1972

HASKELL HOUSE PUBLISHERS Ltd.

Publishers of Scarce Scholarly Books

280 LAFAYETTE STREET

NEW YORK, N. Y. 10012

Library of Congress Cataloging in Publication Data

Gatty, Alfred, 1813-1903.
    A key to Tennyson's In memoriam.

    Reprint of the 1881 ed.
    1. Tennyson, Alfred Tennyson, Baron, 1809-1892.
In memoriam. I. Title.
PR5562.G3 1972   821'.8   72-139
ISBN 0-8383-1399-X

INTRODUCTION.

IN reading *In Memoriam* one rule must be obeyed, if we would really understand the Poem; and that is, that the following most excellent advice should be attended to and accepted:

"There are two ways of reading an author, with a view of understanding him, namely, critically and sympathetically, and the way of sympathy is by far the better. Hereby we associate ourselves with the mind of the writer, penetrate, as it were, behind the scene, and find out his meaning from within outwards. The critical reader, however, who may lack sympathy, approaches his author from the outside, and it is ten to one that he never arrives at the core of the question."[a]

----

[a] This is the advice of an anonymous writer in *Notes and Queries*, and it specially applies to a profitable reading of Holy Scripture.

Nothing can be truer than this judgment, as applied to the works of our modern metaphysical Poets, of whom Tennyson is the chief. The descriptive poetry of a bygone generation is always plain and intelligible; but the inner life, with which the Poet Laureate principally deals, is hidden except to those who would spiritually recognize it.

Is it too much to say that, until one has suffered some acute bereavement, *In Memoriam* is apt to be a sealed volume? The following notes would testify that, since my home was darkened by death, the Poem has been a sublime resource and consolation.

Quite recently I was talking to a dignitary of the Church, who told me that he had turned from *In Memoriam* as a morbid lament which he thought was unnatural; but when he lost a favourite brother, he found that every word suited and soothed his own grief.

No great Poem has ever been more frequently misinterpreted. A most worthy Bishop and fine scholar, now dead, once asked me whether I thought it was Christian! My only reply to such a question would be, that I think it the finest religious Poem in the English language.

I heard the Bishop of Manchester deliver a very able address on the subjects of "Reason and Faith;" and he concluded his oration by quoting from *In Memoriam* such definitions of both as are nowhere else so well expressed.

The Poet Laureate, and many others, may possibly think my comments superflous and often faulty; but the compilation has afforded me high converse with the Unseen, to which I am looking forward; and probably some, who take up this little volume, will have to wait for their own trial, before they can give it a fair judgment.

It is offered as a book of reference only: not as a substitute for the Poem itself; but merely as a translation, to be consulted when the original puzzles the reader's mind.

The purport of some of the passages is so obscure, one might suspect that even the author himself could not exactly determine what he meant when he wrote them. He might possibly require the associations to recur which then affected him; just as Napoleon, when asked whether he would repeat a certain cavalry charge, if he had to fight the battle over again, replied, that he must be placed in the same circumstances to decide.

I myself first read *In Memoriam* with her, who is

> " Now the most blessed memory of mine age."

I have discussed it with many persons, and notably so one evening at Cambridge, in the rooms of a friend who is now a Bishop, when some able and ardent admirers of the Poem were present; and we should certainly have found that my " Key " was useful.

I would record my thanks for the loan of an annotated copy of the Poem, belonging to my friend Mr. Whitmell, H.M. Inspector of Schools, as it has confirmed my own impressions, and added to my views of the subject.

The earnestness and piety of the Poem are indisputable, and for deep thought and reverent speculation on that most important and absorbing of all topics, the condition after death

> "That undiscovered country from whose bourne
> No traveller returns"—

I do not know its equal; since it is the confession of a great mind, laying itself bare to the general eye more candidly and truthfully than I can elsewhere find. It is a tale of sorrow over the loss of a dear friend, who has glided away into the darkness of death; and the Poet struggles with the mystery of this sudden removal of one, who was young, and gifted, and full of promise of a noble life. It is the trouble of Tennyson's own youth that they are thus abruptly parted; and he flings his thoughts loose into the boldest of all questions, "What is this life, and wherefore was it given?"

Whilst superficially regarded, such enquiries may seem to be presumptuous and wrong. The Christian has a Revelation, all sufficient and satisfying for the common death-lists in the daily newspapers. These record the departure of strangers, about whom we are not concerned, for they make no gap in our lives; but when our nearest and dearest are removed, the case is very different; the consolations of the highest Faith then amount to no more than this—that we must submit to remain in ignorance of what has actually befallen those who have left us. In vain we cry with another Poet,

> "Tell us, ye dead ! will none of you in pity
> To those you left behind disclose the secret ;
> O that some courteous ghost would blab it out
> What 'tis you are, and we must shortly be.

The curtain remains drawn, and we can only trust, and be content to know, that the soul is cared for somewhere else.

What is biographical in this Poem is soon summarized.   Alfred Tennyson, a son of the Rev. Dr. Tennyson, rector of Somersby, near Spilsby, in Lincolnshire, was born there in 1809, and in or about 1828, he commenced a close friendship at Trinity College, Cambridge, with Arthur H. Hallam, who was two years his junior, and a son of Henry Hallam, the eminent historian. Both were young men of the highest culture, and one of them, at least, of the highest genius. Their friendship was not founded on a common participation in the ordinary interests of youth; but they sympathised in poetical temperament and philosophical taste. The mental stature of Hallam, and his pure and beautiful disposition in their undergraduate life, are recalled by the Poet in many places, but especially in Poems cix. and following.

In 1829, the two friends competed for the Chancellor's gold medal for the English Prize Poem, the subject being " Timbuctoo," and Tennyson gained it. This College intimacy was continued at both their homes, and Hallam became engaged in marriage to one of Tennyson's sisters. This alliance may have deepened the attachment of the friends, but was not needed to account for the survivor writing of the departed as " more than my brothers are to me."

Kinship does not necessarily ensure our deepest affection. On the contrary, we leave the family in which we were born, to make a new home of our own, when we have met and married one who was previously a stranger to us ; and so we may be sure that *In Memoriam* was written before the Poet had a wife. The intense and romantic affection which it expresses was the outpouring of friendship conceived in the heart before it had realized the higher love. This explanation seems to me to excuse and

 INTRODUCTION.

justify the warmth of sentiment which prevails throughout the Poem, where I find more of the reality of grief than I can discover in either the "Sonnets" of Shakespeare, or the "Lycidas" of Milton, to both of which it has often been compared. It is more like the Book of Job than either of these.

The circumstances attending the death of Arthur Hallam were singularly painful. He had taken his degree at Cambridge, was reading Law at the Temple, and in the early autumn of 1833 accompanied his father in a brief continental tour; and on the 15th September they were at Vienna, when a sudden rush of blood to the head put an instantaneous end to Arthur Hallam's life. As Tennyson speaks of this event—

"God's finger touch'd him and he slept."

The body was afterwards brought to England, and on 3rd January, 1834, was buried in Clevedon Church, on the Severn, where was the seat of his maternal uncle, Sir Charles Abraham Elton, Bart.

The shock of this sudden bereavement on Tennyson's sensitive nature found expression in the Poem we are considering. We know, from internal evidence, that it was not written off at once, but was the cherished work of several years; being continued throughout that period of life when the feelings and affections are most susceptible, when 'our place in the world is not yet fixed, and when the contemplative and anxious are encountering most difficulties and trials.

The introductory stanzas, which contain a summary of the Poet's faith, are dated 1849, and the Poem was published in 1850. There was, therefore, a long interval between Hallam's death and the date of publication; and it is probable that other influences deepened the sorrowing spirit of the writer whilst employed at his intermitted task. We will, for the present, leave the introductory stanzas, as, like other prefaces, they were no doubt last written.

In order that I may be clearly understood, I must explain that each division, containing a varying number of stanzas in this grand monologue of grief, will be called a " Poem."

" Moderate lamentation is the right of the dead,
Excessive grief the enemy to the living."

All's well that ends well, Act i., s. 1.

KEY TO TENNYSON'S "IN MEMORIAM."

I.

IT may be stated, on the highest authority, that the Poet alluded to in the opening stanza, cannot be identified.

St. Augustine wrote, that we can rise higher on the ladder of life, by trampling down our vices. His words, in a Sermon on the Ascension, are, *De vitiis nostris scalam nobis facimus, si vitia ipsa calcamus.*

Longfellow published a Poem, not earlier than 1842, which he called "The Ladder of St. Augustine;" and more recently, Lowell, another American Poet, has adopted the same idea—or rather, a similar one—when he says,

> " 'Tis sorrow builds the shining ladder up,
> Whose golden rounds are our calamities,
> Whereon our feet firm planting, nearer God
> The spirit climbs, and hath its eyes unseal'd."

The "dead selves" of Tennyson are neither our vices nor our calamities; but, rather, our general experiences, which all perish as they happen; and of these, in his own case, the special loss he had sustained in the death of Hallam (his "more than brother"— his *dimidium sui*, "bosom-friend and half of life") should rouse him to soar into "higher things;" rather than leave him to be pointed at, as "the man that loved and lost" (see Poems xxvii., 4, and lxxxv., 1); and all that he had before been, as now "overworn," and prostrated, by this one bereavement.

But it was difficult to anticipate in the future a gain to match the loss he had sustained; and to appropriate interest, *i.e.*, reap the fruit of tears that he was now shedding. Love, however, shall uphold his grief with sustaining power; for it is better to be grief-mad, and " dance with death "— (singing and dancing being a custom at ancient funerals)—than become a spectacle of scorn for " the victor Hours" to deride, after they have effaced his love-born sorrow.

II.

But the struggle back to past contentment and happiness is difficult; and the "Old Yew" of the church-yard seems to typify his present state of feeling.

Its root and fibres stretch downward, and hold the scull and bones of the dead; like as his thoughts cling to his departed friend. Its "dusk" or shadow is before the church clock, which strikes the hours of mortality, and this harmonizes with his life of mourning.

The tree preserves its "thousand years of gloom," unchanged by the seasons which affect other things—the "old yew" continues always the same—

> " And gazing on thee, sullen tree,
>   I seem to fail from out my blood
> And grow incorporate into thee."

It would almost seem as if the Poet, whose scientific allusions are always so striking and correct, was not aware, when he wrote this Poem, that the yew bore blossom and seed, like other trees.

Hence, his recent introduction of Poem xxxix.; also the description, near the beginning of "The Holy Grail"—

> " They sat
> Beneath a world-old yew tree, darkening half
> The cloisters, on a gustful April morn
> That puff'd the swaying branches into smoke.
>   O, brother, I have seen this yew tree smoke,
> Spring after spring, for half a hundred years."

It will be seen, in the later Poem, how a comparison with the gloomy yew has been modified.

III.

"Sorrow, cruel fellowship," from which he cannot disengage himself, now reigns within him, and distorts with "lying lip" all Nature and her beneficent workings; making these seem to have no purpose or end. All which is but an echo of his own dark feelings. Shall he then believe this false guide—

> "Embrace her as my natural good;
> Or crush her, like a vice of blood,
> Upon the threshold of the mind?"

reject, and turn away from the impostures of a sorrowing imagination?

IV.

In sleep there is no struggle of the will; and he communes with his own heart, which is beating so low; a condition that must be caused by a sense of "something lost."

"Break," he says, still addressing his heart, but in metaphor;

> "Break, thou deep vase of chilling tears,
> That grief hath shaken into frost."

This must refer to the scientific fact, that water can be lowered in temperature below the freezing point, without solidifying; but it expands at once into ice if disturbed; and the suddenness of the expansion breaks the containing vessel.[a]

Clouds of undefined trouble, such as "dreams are made of," pass "below the darken'd eyes," that is, figure themselves on the brain under the eyelids; but on awaking, the will reasserts its power, and protests against the folly of such mourning. He would therefore dismiss the phantom, Sorrow.

[a] Shakespeare says,
> "My heart is turn'd to stone;
> I strike it, and it hurts my hand."
> *Othello*, Act iv., s. 1.

V.

He sometimes hesitates, as at something half sinful, when giving expression to his sadness; because words at best only partially declare what the Soul feels; just as outward Nature cannot fully display the inner life.

But "after all" words act like narcotics, and numb pain; so, like putting on the garb of mourning, he will wrap himself over in words; although these, like coarse clothes on the body, give no more than an outline of his "large grief."

VI.

The "common" expressions of sympathy with our trouble are very "common-place"—

"Vacant chaff well meant for grain."

A friend asks, "Why grieve?" "Other friends remain;" "Loss is common to the race;" as Hamlet says, "All that lives must die." Is this comfort? rather the contrary. We know it is so—

> "Never morning wore
> To evening, but some heart did break."

The father drinks his son's health at the war, in the moment when that son is shot.

The mother prays for her sailor-boy, when

> "His heavy-shotted hammock-shroud
> Drops in his vast and wandering grave."

The girl is dressing before the glass, and strives to array herself most becomingly for her expected lover; and he meanwhile is either drowned in the ford, or killed by a fall from his horse—

> "O what to her shall be the end?
>   And what to me remains of good?
>   To her perpetual maidenhood,
> And unto me no second friend,"

There is a fine passage in J. Taylor's "Holy Dying," which contains a like rumination on the uncertainty of life. "The wild fellow in *Petronius* that escaped upon a broken table from the furies of a shipwreck, as he was sunning himself upon the rocky shore, espied a man rolled upon his floating bed of waves, ballasted with sand in the folds of his garments, and carried by his civil enemy the sea towards the shore to find a grave; and it cast him into some sad thoughts; that peradventure this man's wife in some part of the Continent, safe and warm, looks next month for the good man's return; or it may be his son knows nothing of the tempest; or his father thinks of that affectionate kiss which still is warm upon the good old man's cheek ever since he took a kind fare-well, and he weeps with joy to think how blessed he shall be when his beloved boy returns into the circle of his father's arms.

"These are the thoughts of mortals, this is the end and sum of all their designs; a dark night and an ill guide, a boisterous sea and a broken cable, an hard rock and a rough wind dashed in pieces the fortune of a whole family, and they that shall weep loudest for the accident, are not yet entered into the storm, and yet have suffered shipwreck."

VII.

He persists in indulging his melancholy, and so creeps, "like a guilty thing," at early morning to the door of the house in London where Hallam had lived — probably in Wimpole Street—but this only serves to remind him that

"He is not here; but far away."

The revival of busy movement on a

wet morning in a dull London street,
is vividly described—

> " The noise of life begins again,
> And ghastly thro' the drizzling rain
> On the bald street breaks the blank day."

VIII.

He next compares himself to the
disappointed lover who "alights" from
his horse, calls at the home of his
mistress,

> " And learns her gone and far from home."

So, as the disappointed lover, to whom
the whole place has at once become
dismal, wanders into the garden, and
culls a now rain-beaten flower, which
she had once fostered; even thus will
he cherish and plant "this poor flower
of poesy" on Hallam's tomb, because
his friend when alive was pleased with
his verses.

IX.

This Poem commences an address

to the ship that brings Hallam's body from Vienna to Bristol—

> "My lost Arthur's loved remains."

No words can be more touching than his appeal to the vessel, for care and tenderness in transporting its precious freight.   He bids it come quickly; "spread thy full wings," hoist every sail; "ruffle thy mirror'd mast"; for the faster the ship is driven through the water, the more will the reflected mast be "ruffled" on its agitated surface.   May no rude wind "perplex thy sliding keel," until Phosphor the morning star, Venus, shines; and during the night may the lights above and the winds around be gentle as the sleep of him—

> "My Arthur, whom I shall not see
>   Till all my widow'd race be run;"

until my life, bereaved of its first affection, be over.

In Poem xvii., 5, the same line occurs—"Till all my widow'd race be run," and it agrees with St. Paul's declaration, 2 Tim., iv., 7, "I have finished my course." The words *race* and *course* are synonymous, and refer to the foot-races of the ancients. "More than my brothers are to me," is repeated in P. lxxix., 1.

X.

Very beautifully is the picture continued of the ship's passage, and he appeals to it for safely conducting

> "Thy dark freight, a vanish'd life."

The placid scene, which he had imagined as attending the vessel, harmonizes with the home-bred fancy, that it is sweeter

> "To rest beneath the clover sod,
>   That takes the sunshine and the rains;"

that is, to be buried in the open churchyard;

> " Or where the kneeling hamlet drains
> The chalice of the grapes of God," [a]

that is, in the chancel of the church, near the altar rails; than if, together with the ship, "the roaring wells" of the sea

> " Should gulf him fathom-deep in brine ;
> And hands so often clasp'd in mine,
> Should toss with tangle and with shells."

"Tangle," or "oar-weed," *Laminaria digitata*, says the Algologist, "is never met with but at extreme tide-limits, where some of its broad leather-like fronds may be seen darkly overhanging the rocks, while others, a little lower down, are rising and dipping in the water like sea-serpents floated by the waves."

XI.

This Poem would describe a calm and quiet day in October — late autumn.

[a] This fruit of the vine, Matt. xxvi., 29.

It is said that the scenery sketched does not accord with that of Clevedon. Will it suit Somersby any better? Surely, near the Lincolnshire coast these features might be found :

" Calm and still light on yon great plain
    That sweeps with all its autumn bowers,
    And crowded farms and lessening towers,
To mingle with the bounding main."

The effect of distance would be, to bring the scattered farms in nearer contiguity, and to lessen the height of the church towers, until they all seemed to mingle with the sea beyond.

The stillness is just broken by the sound of the horse chestnut falling through the dead leaves, and these are reddening to their own fall. No time of the year is more quiet, not even is the insect abroad : the waves just swell and fall noiselessly, and this reminds him of

> " The dead calm in that noble breast
> Which heaves but with the heaving deep."

XII.

An ecstacy follows : in which the soul of the Poet seems to mount, like a dove rising into the heavens with a message of woe tied under her wings ; and so the disembodied soul leaves its " mortal ark "—" our earthly house of this tabernacle "—(2 Cor. v., 1) and flees away

> " O'er ocean-mirrors rounded large "

(the sea line constantly expanding and always being circular), until it reaches the ship, on whose margin it settles, weeping with the piteous cry—

> " Is this the end of all my care?
> Is this the end?   Is this the end?"

Then it seems to

> " return
> To where the body sits, and learn,
> That I have been an hour away."

XIII.

The tears shed by the widower, when he wakes from a dream of his deceased wife, and " moves his doubtful arms" to find her place empty; are like the tears he himself is weeping over "a loss for ever new," a terrible void where there had been social intercourse, and a "silence" that will never be broken. For he is lamenting

> "the comrade of my choice,
> An awful thought, a life removed,
> The human-hearted man I loved,
> A Spirit, not a breathing voice."

Hallam is now only a remembrance —no longer endowed with bodily functions, and the survivor cannot quite accept what has happened.

He therefore asks Time to teach him the real truth, and make him feel that these strange things, over which his tears are shed, are not merely

a prolonged dream; and he begs
that his fancies, hovering over the
approaching ship, may quite realise
that it brings no ordinary freight, but
actually the mortal remains of his
friend.

The difficulty in apprehending his
complete loss is further shown by
his address to the ship, saying, that
if it had arrived in port, and he saw
the passengers step across the plank
to shore; and amongst them came
Hallam himself, and they renewed all
their former friendship; and Hallam,
unchanged in every respect, heard his
tale of sorrow with surprise:

"I should not feel it to be strange."

Both this and the previous Poem
express the difficulty we feel in
realising the death of some one who
is dear to us. So Cowper wrote, after
losing his mother, and in expectation
that she would yet return:

> "What ardently I wish'd, I still believed,
> And disappointed still, was still deceived."

A stormy change in the weather occurs: the winds "roar from yonder dropping day," that is, from the west, into which the daylight is sinking. And all the sights and sounds of tempest alarm him for the safety of the ship, and

> "But for fancies which aver
>   That all thy motions gently pass
>   Athwart a plane of molten glass,
> I scarce could brook the strain and stir," &c.

all the symptoms of storm indicated by a fiery sunset.

In Job xxxvii., 18, we read, "Hast thou with him spread out the sky, which is strong, and as a molten looking glass?"

XVI.

This Poem is highly metaphysical. He asks whether Sorrow, which is his abiding feeling, can be such a changeling as to alternate in his breast betwixt " calm despair " (see P. xi., 4) and " wild unrest ? " (see P. xv., 4) ; or does she only just take this " touch of change," as calm or storm prevails ? having no more of even transient form, than what a lake holds in " the shadow of a lark," when reflected on its surface.

Being distinct from bodily pain, Sorrow is more like the reflection than the thing reflected. But the shock he has received has made his mind confused, and he is like a ship that strikes on a rock and founders. He becomes a

> " delirous man,
> Whose fancy fuses old and new,
> And flashes into false and true,
> And mingles all without a plan." a

XVII.

He hails the ship—" thou comest "

a See 2 Cor. xii., 2.

—and feels as if his own whispered prayer for its safety, had been wafting it steadily across the sea. In spirit, he had seen it move

    " thro' circles of the bounding sky "—

the horizon at sea being always circular (see P. xii., 3)—and he would wish its speedy arrival, inasmuch as it brings "all I love."

For doing this, he invokes a blessing upon all its future voyages. It is now bringing

> " The dust of him I shall not see
> Till all my widow'd race be run." [a]

XVIII.

The ship arrives, the "dear remains" are landed, and the burial takes place.

It is something, worth the mourner's having, that he can stand on English ground where his friend has been laid, and that the violet will spring from his ashes.

[a] See P. ix., 5, and P. lxxxv., 29.

Hamlet says of Ophelia,

> " Lay her in the earth
> And from her fair and unpolluted flesh
> May violets spring ! "

A beautiful invitation follows to those, who are sometimes irreverent bearers :

> " Come then, pure hands, and bear the head
> That sleeps or wears the mask of sleep,
> And come, whatever loves to weep,
> And hear the ritual of the dead."

Even yet, before the grave is closed, he would like, as Elisha did on the Shunamite woman's child, to cast himself, and

> " thro' his lips impart
> The life that almost dies in me ; "

but still he resolves to form the firmer resolution and to submit; though meanwhile treasuring the look and words that are past and gone for ever.

XIX.

From the Danube to the Severn—from Vienna to Bristol—the body had been conveyed, and was interred on the banks of the latter river, where the village of Clevedon stands.

The Wye, a tributary of the Severn, is also tidal; and when deepened by the sea flowing inward, its babbling ceases; but the noise recurs when the sea flows back.

So does the Poet's power of expressing his grief alternate: at times he is too full in heart to find utterance; but after awhile, as when "the wave again is vocal in its wooded" banks,

> " My deeper anguish also falls,
> And I can speak a little then."

XX.

He knows both the "lesser grief" and the "deeper anguish:" his spirits are thus variably affected.

In his lighter mood, he laments as servants mourn for a good master who has died:

> "It will be hard, they say, to find
> Another service such as this."

But he is also visited by a sense of deeper deprivation, such as children feel when they lose a father, and

> "see the vacant chair, and think,
> How good! how kind! and he is gone."

XXI.

This Poem opens as if Hallam's grave was in the churchyard, where grasses waved; but it was not so, he was buried inside Clevedon church.

The Poet imagines the reproofs, with which passers by will visit him for his unrestrained grief. He would "make weakness weak:" would parade his pain to court sympathy, and gain credit for constancy; and another says, that a display of private sorrow is quite inappropriate at times, when great political changes impend, and Science every month is evolving some new secret.

He replies, that his song is but like that of the linnet — joyous indeed when her brood first flies, but sad when the nest has been rifled of her young.

XXII.

For "four sweet years," from flowery spring to snowy winter, they had lived in closest friendship ;

> "But where the path we walk'd began
>   To slant the fifth autumnal slope,"

"the Shadow fear'd of man," grim death, "broke our fair companionship."

Hallam died on the 15th September, 1833, and the survivor, eagerly pursuing, can find him no more, but

> "thinks, that somewhere in the waste
> The Shadow sits and waits for me."

His own spirit becomes darkened by gloomy apprehensions.

XXIII.

Feeling his extreme loneliness, he

wanders sometimes to where the cloaked Shadow sits, Death,

"Who keeps the keys of all the creeds"—

inasmuch as only when we die shall we know the whole truth ; and "falling lame" on his way, that is, stumbling in his vain enquiries as to whence he came and whither he is going, he can only grasp one feeling, which is, that all is miserably changed since they were in company—friends enjoying life together, and indulging in scholarly communion.

XXIV.

But, after all, was their happiness perfect ? No, the very sun, the "fount of Day," has spots on its surface— "wandering isles of night." If all had been wholly good and fair, this earth would have remained the Paradise it has never looked, "since Adam left his garden," as appears in the earlier editions; but now the line runs,

" Since our first Sun arose and set."

Does " the haze of grief " then magnify the past, as things look larger in a fog?[a] Or does his present lowness of spirits set the past in relief, as projections are more apparent when you are beneath them? Or is the past from being far off always in glory, as distance lends enchantment to the view; and so the world becomes orbed

" into the perfect star
We saw not, when we moved therein ? "

We are told that, if we were placed in the moon, we should see the Earth as—" the perfect star "—having a shining surface, and being thirteen times larger than the moon itself.

[a] The effect of vapour in magnifying objects is shown towards the end of the Idyll, "Guinevere," where it says :

"The moony vapour rolling round the King,
Who seem'd the phantom of a Giant in it."

XXV.

All he knows is, that whilst with Hallam, there was life.   They went side by side, and upheld the daily burden.

He himself moved light as a carrier bird in air, and delighted in the weight he bore because Love shared it ; and he transferred half of every pain to his dear companion, so that he himself was never weary in either heart or limb.

XXVI.

Dismal and dreary as life has become, he nevertheless wishes to live, if only to prove the stedfastness of his affection.   And he asks that if the all-seeing Eye, which already perceives the future rottenness of the living tree, and the far off ruin of the now standing tower, can detect any coming indifference in him — any failure of Love — then may the "Shadow waiting with the keys" "shroud me from my proper scorn;"a hide me from my own self-contempt!

"In Him is no before." Jehovah is simply, *I am*, to whom foresight and foreknowledge cannot be attributed, since past and future are equally present.

The morn breaks over Indian seas, because they are to the east of us.

XXVII.

He neither envies the cage-born bird "that never knew the summer woods," and is content without liberty; nor the beast that lives uncontrolled by conscience; nor the heart that never loved; " nor any want-begotten rest," that is repose arising from defective sensibility.

a "My proper scorn"—*proprius*—is scorn of myself, an imprecation. See Lancelot's self-condemnation at the end of "Lancelot and Elaine."

On the contrary,

> " I hold it true, whate'er befall ;
> I feel it, when I sorrow most ;
> 'Tis better to have loved and lost
> Than never to have loved at all."

Seneca in Epistle 99 says, *Magis gauderes quod habueras, quam mœreres quod amiseras.*—See P. lxxxv., 1.

The Poem seems to halt here and begin afresh, with a description of Christmastide.

XXVIII.

Christmas Eve at Somersby, and most probably at the end of the year 1834.

Throughout this first year of his bereavement, he may have "slept and woke with pain," and almost wished he might never more hear the Christmas bells.

But a calmer spirit has now come over him: he listens to the Christmas peals rung at four neighbouring churches, and the sound soothes him with tender associations :

> " But they my troubled spirit rule,
>   For they controll'd me when a boy ;
>   They bring me sorrow touch'd with joy,
>   The merry merry bells of Yule."

Yule is Christmas, and the word may be derived from *Jubilum*, being the jubilee which brings glad tidings of great joy to all people.

XXIX.

Having such " compelling cause to grieve " over the decease of Hallam, how can they venture to keep Christmas Eve as usual ? He is absent, who when amongst them was so eminently social. But it must be done. " Use and wont," " old sisters of a day gone by," still demand what has been customary. " They too will die," and new habits succeed.

To the fourteenth chapter of Walter Scott's " Pirate," there is the following motto from "Old Play," which meant Scott's own invention :

> " We'll keep our customs. What is law itself
> But old establish'd custom ? What religion
> (I mean with one half of the men that use it)
> Save the good use and wont that carries them
> To worship how and where their fathers
>   worshipp'd ?
> All things resolve to custom. We'll keep ours."

XXX.

The Christian festival proceeds, and there is the family gathering, with such games as are common at this season ; but sadness weighs on all, for they entertain "an awful sense of one mute shadow" — Hallam's wraith— being present and watching them.

They sit in silence, then break into singing

> " A merry song we sang with him
> Last year."

This identifies the time to be Christmas, 1834.

They comfort themselves with the conviction that the dead retain "their mortal sympathy," and still feel with those they have left behind. The soul, a "keen seraphic flame," pierces

"From orb to orb, from veil to veil,"

and so traverses the universe.

Was the anniversary of our Saviour's birth ever hailed in terms more sublime and beautiful !

"Rise, happy morn, rise, holy morn,
    Draw forth the cheerful day from night:
    O Father, touch the east, and light
The light that shone when Hope was born."

XXXI.

The mind of the Poet has now taken a more strictly religious view of the situation; and he would like to learn the secrets of the grave from the experience of Lazarus.

Did Lazarus in death yearn to hear his sister Mary weeping for him ?   If she asked him, when restored to life, where he was during his four days of entombment ;

> " There lives no record of reply,"

which, if given, might have " added praise to praise "—that is, might have sealed and confirmed the promise that " blessed are the dead which die in the Lord."

As it was, the neighbours met and offered congratulations, and their cry was,

> " Behold a man raised up by Christ !
>   The rest remaineth unreveal'd ;
>   He told it not ; or something seal'd
> The lips of that Evangelist."

It is only St. John who records the miracle.

XXXII.

Mary's eyes, looking alternately at her brother who had been restored to life, and at our Lord who had revived

him, are "homes of silent prayer;"
and one strong affection overpowers
every other sentiment, when her
"ardent gaze" turns from the face
of Lazarus, "and rests upon the Life"
—Christ, the author and giver of life.

Her whole spirit is then so "borne
down by gladness," that

> "She bows, she bathes the Saviour's feet
> With costly spikenard and with tears."

No lives are so blessed as those which
consist of "faithful prayers:" no at-
tachments so enduring as those which
are based on the higher love of God.

But are there any souls so pure as
to have reached this higher range of
feeling; or if there be, what blessed-
ness can equal theirs?

XXXIII.

This Poem is abstruse, and requires
thought and care for the interpretation
of the Poet's meaning.

It seems to be an address of warning and reproof to a moral pantheist, who fancies that he has attained a higher and purer air, by withholding his faith from all " form," and recognising Deity in everything—his faith having " centre everywhere."

This sceptic is warned from disturbing the pious woman, who is happy in her prayers to a personal God ; for they bring an " early heaven " on her life.   Her faith is fixed on " form ; " and to flesh and blood she has linked a truth divine, by seeing God incarnate in the person of Christ.

The pantheist must take care for himself, that, whilst satisfied

> " In holding by the law within,"

the guidance of his own reason, he does not after all fail in a sinful world, " for want of such a type," as the life of Christ on earth affords.

XXXIV.

His own dim consciousness should teach him thus much, that Life will never be extinguished. Else all here is but dust and ashes. The earth and sun are but "fantastic beauty"—such as a wild Poet might invent, who has neither conscience nor aim.

Even God can be nothing to the writer, if all around him is doomed to perish; and he will not himself wait in patience, but rather "sink to peace;" and, like the birds that are charmed by the serpent into its mouth, he will "drop head-foremost in the jaws of vacant darkness," and so cease to exist.

XXXV.

And yet, if a trustworthy voice from the grave should testify, that there is no life beyond this world, even then he would endeavour to keep alive so sweet a thing as Love, during this brief mortal existence.

But still there would sound

" The moanings of the homeless sea,"

and of streams disintegrating and washing down the rocks to form future land surfaces—" Æonian hills," the formations of whole æons being thus dissolved — and Love itself would languish under

" The sound of that forgetful shore,"

the banks of Lethe—knowing that its own death was impending.

But the case is idly put. If Death were from the first seen as it is when it comes, Love would either not exist, or would be a mere fellowship of coarse appetites, like those of the Satyr, who crushes the grape for drunken revelry, and basks and battens in the woods.

XXXVI.

Although, even in manhood, the great truths of Religion only

"darkly join,
Deep-seated in our mystic frame,"

since at best we only see as through
a glass darkly: we nevertheless bless
His name, who "made them current
coin," so as to be generally intelligible.
This was done by the teaching of
Parables.

For Divine Wisdom, having to deal
with mortal powers, conveyed sacred
truth through "lowly doors," by em-
bodying it in earthly similitudes;
because "closest words" will not
explain Divine things, owing to the
imperfection of human language;
"and so the Word had breath,"
"God was manifest in the flesh" (1
Tim. iii., 16, and 1 John, 14), and by
good works wrought the best of all
creeds, which the labourer in the field,
the mason, the grave-digger,

"And those wild eyes that watch the wave
In roarings round the coral reef,"

even the savages of the Pacific Islands, can see and understand, being conveyed to them through the parables of the Gospel.

XXXVII.

He imagines Urania, the heavenly Muse, to reprove him for venturing on sacred ground, and commenting on religious themes; as she would have him confine his steps to his own Parnassus, and there earn the laurel crown.

But his own tragic muse, Melpomene, replies with the apology, that though unworthy to speak of holy mysteries, yet with his earthly song he had striven to soothe his own aching heart, and render a due tribute to human love; and inasmuch as the comfort he had drawn was "clasp'd in truth reveal'd" had its foundation in the Gospel : he daringly

> " loiter'd in the Master's field,
> And darken'd sanctities with song."

Many readers of *In Memoriam* will have thanked its author for these trespasses upon the Holy Land, feeling indeed there was no profane intrusion.

Some will regret that he has changed the original line, "and dear as sacramental wine," into "and dear to me as sacred wine :" the purpose, one supposes, was that the reader should see that he spoke only for himself—"to me"—the meaning is unchanged, but the sound is rather flat.

XXXVIII.

The sadness of his heart has fully returned, and the journey of life is dull and weary. The skies above and the prospect before him are no longer what they used to be, when Hallam was by. "The blowing season," when

the equinoctial gales of March are
raging: the "herald melodies of
spring," when the birds proclaim that
winter is past, give him no joy; but
in his own songs he finds a "gleam
of solace;" and if after death there
be any consciousness retained of what
has been left upon earth,

> "Then are these songs I sing of thee
> Not all ungrateful to thine ear."

XXXIX.

This Poem has been recently introduced, and, as already stated (see P. ii.),
seems designed to shew that the Poet
was desirous not to convey a wrong
impression of the nature of the yew
tree.   It does really blossom, and
form fruit and seed like other trees,
though few may have noticed this.

He now says that his "random
stroke" on the tree brings off

> "Fruitful cloud and living smoke;"

Also that at the proper season

" Thy gloom is kindled at the tips."

The fact is, that the flower is bright yellow in colour, but very minute; and when the tree is shaken, the pollen comes off like dust, and then the tree seems to resume its old gloom.

So the spirit of the Poet may brighten for a moment, and then return to its accustomed melancholy.

XL.

He wishes "the widow'd hour" could be forgotten, or rather recalled like an occasion when the bride leaves her first home for " other realms of love." There are tears then, but April tears —rain and sunshine mixed ; and as the bride's future office may be to rear and teach another generation— uniting grand-parents with grand-children—so he has no doubt that to Hallam

> " is given
> A life that bears immortal fruit
> In such great offices as suit
> The full-grown energies of heaven."

But then comes this difference. The bride will return in course of time with her baby, and all at her old home will be happier for her absence —whereas

> " thou and I have shaken hands,
> Till growing winters lay me low;
> My paths are in the fields I know,
> But thine in undiscover'd lands."

XLI.

Whilst together upon earth they could advance in company, though Hallam's spirit and intellect were ever soaring upwards. Now the links which united them are lost, and he can no longer partake in his friend's transformations. So, (folly though it be,) he wishes that, by an effort of will, he could

"leap the grades of life and light,
And flash at once, my friend, to thee."

See P. xcv., 9.

For, though he has no vague dread of death and "the gulfs beneath," yet the chilling thought comes over him, that in death he may not be able to overtake his friend, but evermore remain "a life behind" him,

"Through all the secular to be"—

all future ages: and that so he shall be his mate no more, which is his great trouble.

"The howlings of forgotten fields"

is probably a classical allusion to those "fields" of mystic horror, over which the spirits of the departed were supposed to range, uttering wild shrieks and cries. Has Dante no such allusion?

This Poem intimates the idea of progress and advancement after death.

XLII.

He reproaches himself for these fancies ; for inasmuch as it was only unity of place which gave them the semblance of equality here—Hallam being always really ahead—why may not " Place retain us still," and I be trained and taught anew by this "lord of large experience ? "

> " And what delights can equal those
>   That stir the spirit's inner deeps,
>   When one that loves but knows not, reaps
> A truth from one that loves and knows ? "

There are no pleasures so sweet, as the imbibings of instruction from the lips of those who are both superior and dear to us.

XLIII.

If, in the intermediate state, we find that

> " Sleep and Death be truly one "—

as St. Paul himself might lead us to believe—

" And every spirit's folded bloom "

—the slumbering soul being like a flower which closes at night—reposed, unconscious of the passage of time, but with silent traces of the past marked upon it; then the lives of all, from the beginning of time, would contain in their shut up state a record of all that had ever happened ;

> " And love would last as pure and whole,
>   As when he loved me here in Time,
>   And at the spiritual prime
> Rewaken with the dawning soul."

At the resurrection the old affection will revive.

XLIV.

How fare the happy dead ?   Here man forgets what happened

> " before
> God shut the doorways of his head ; "

that is, before the skull of the infant closed.   Yet sometimes

"A little flash, a mystic hint"

suggests the possibility of a previous existence.[a]

And so, "in the long harmonious years" of death, some dim touch of earthly things may reach Hallam whilst ranging with his equals. If this should be allowed, "O turn thee round" and listen to my guardian angel, who will tell thee all about us here.

XLV.

The child, still in its mother's arms, has no consciousness of its own

---

[a] Wordsworth entertains the notion of our having lived before in his fine Ode, "Intimations of Immortality," wherein be says,

"Our birth is but a sleep and a forgetting :
The soul that rises with us, our life's star,
  Hath elsewhere had its setting,
And cometh from afar," &c.

Tennyson also says in "The Two Voices :"

"Moreover, something is or seems,
That touches me with mystic gleams,
Like glimpses of forgotten dreams—

Of something felt, like something here ;
Of something done, I know not where ;
Such as no language may declare."

individual life and identity; and it is with its growth that it acquires a sense of separate and isolated being, independent of all around.

The acquisition of this consciousness may be the use of "blood and breath," which otherwise would have achieved no worthy end; as we should have to learn ourselves afresh after the second birth of death, if they had not assured us of our indisputable personality.

XLVI.

In this life we experience "thorn and flower," grief and joy; and the past becomes mercifully shaded as time goes on, otherwise the retrospect would be intolerable. But hereafter all shadow on what has happened will be removed, and all will be "clear from marge to marge;" and the five years of earthly friendship will be the "richest field," in the "eternal landscape."

Yet this would be a limited range for Love, which ought to extend without any circumscription,

"A rosy warmth from marge to marge,"

its expansion interminable.

XLVII.

This great and religious Poem has been absurdly said to teach Pantheism, which these stanzas refute; or perhaps they rather deny the doctrine of Spinoza, if that be clearly understood.

At any rate, to be conscious of "a separate whole"—a distinct individuality—and yet merge at last

"in the general Soul,
Is faith as vague as all unsweet:
Eternal form shall still divide
The eternal soul from all beside;
And I shall know him when we meet." [a]

[a] When Mrs. Alfred Gatty died, a lady of rank and high character showed great interest in the event. She requested me to call upon her in London, when she expressed her deep gratitude to the author of "Parables from Nature," which had introduced her to new and most serious thoughts. She said, "I never saw Mrs. Gatty, but I shall know her by her writings when we meet hereafter." She did not long survive her unknown friend.—A.G.

St. Paul is not more distinct and emphatic upon our individuality hereafter, when he says, we shall "be clothed upon with our house which is from heaven," 2 Cor. v., 2 ; that is, we shall put on a spiritual *body*, that will give identity and form.

Delighting in the thought of

"Enjoying each the other's good,"

he feels to have attracted the approving Shade of Hallam, and this reluctantly fades away, with the tender parting :

"Farewell, we lose ourselves in light."

XLVIII.

This Poem disclaims any attempt at settling religious difficulties. The verses are "of sorrow born," the result of private grief; and if misunderstood, and open to the charge of attempting to solve such grave questions of doubt as affect some minds, they would deserve the scorn of men.

Sorrow does not undertake severe argument ; but if a "slender shade of doubt" flits before it, it would make it "vassal unto love," and yield to Love's supreme authority.

Love ought to be our ruler and guide, and these lays of sadness are merely

> "Short swallow-flights of song, that dip
> Their wings in tears, and skim away."

XLIX.

He compares the "random influences" of Art, Nature, and the Schools, to light breaking in shivered lances on the dappled water. For even so does "the sullen surface" of the mind become "crisp" and curled with the wave of thought, the eddy of fancy, the air of song.

The transient passenger may look and go on his way, but must not blame such mental perturbations : for

> " Beneath all fancied hopes and fears,
>   Ay me,[a] the sorrow deepens down,
>   Whose muffled motions blindly drown
> The bases of my life in tears."

L.

He invokes Hallam's spirit to be near him in his various moods of distress — when he is filled with nervous apprehensions, when faith seems gone, and Time to be only "a maniac scattering dust," and Life to be "a Fury slinging flame:" when men also appear to be no more than flies, that sting, and weave their cells, and die.   But above all,

> " Be near me when I fade away,
>   To point the term of human strife,
>   And on the low dark verge of life,
> The twilight of eternal day."

The idea is sustained, that we shall go through the darkness of death,

[a] " Ay" must have the force of the Greek $\overset{\smile}{\alpha}\iota$ "alas"— and " ay me " be as the Latin *hei mihi,* " woe is me ! "

when Time will be lost, into the dawning light of Eternity; and the Poet would have his friend be near him at this translation.

LI.

Dare we indeed challenge the dead to inspect us? Have we "no inner vileness" that we would not have them discover? Would the Poet be lessened in Hallam's esteem and affection, when "some hidden shame" was exposed? No,

> " There must be wisdom with great Death :
> The dead shall look me thro' and thro'."
>
> . . . .
>
> " They watch, like God, the rolling hours
> With larger other eyes than ours,
> To make allowance for us all."

LII.

He complains of his own inability to love Hallam as he ought, that is, worthily; because, if he did so, he would be equal to his friend,

" For love reflects the thing beloved ; "

whereas his words are words only, the "froth of thought."

The Spirit of love reproves this self-accusation :

" Thou canst not move me from thy side,
Nor human frailty do me wrong."

There is no ideal of excellence, which we may conceive, that will ensure our attaining to it :

" not the sinless years
That breathed beneath the Syrian blue "—

not the life of Christ, in the clear atmosphere of Palestine, keeps any spirit "wholly true" to that pattern of perfection.

So be not "like an idle girl" fretting over little faults—"flecks of sin." But wait, thy wealth will be gathered in—thy worth shown,

" When Time hath sunder'd shell from pearl "—

when the flesh has left the Soul free from its contaminating influence.

LIII.

He has often known a father, now

"A sober man, among his boys,"

whose youth was noisy and foolish. Are we then to conclude from his example, that had there been no wild oats sown, there scarcely would have come

"The grain by which a man may live?"

If we ventured to name such a doctrine among the old, would we preach it to the young, who still "eddy round and round?"

Hold fast what is good, and define it well; and take care that "divine Philosophy" does not exceed her legitimate bound, and become

"Procuress to the lords of hell"—

by advocating sin as the path to sanctity.

LIV.

This Poem expresses a hope in Universalism—

> " that somehow good
> Will be the final goal of ill "—

that natural propensities, wilful sins, imperfect faith, and inherited weakness, may all find a pardonable solution.

He hopes that nothing has been made in vain—

> " That not one life shall be destroy'd,
> Or cast as rubbish to the void,
> When God hath made the pile complete."

But how reverently does he touch this mysterious subject !

> " Behold, we know not anything ;
> I can but trust that good shall fall
> At last—far off—at last, to all,
> And every winter change to spring.
>
> So runs my dream : but what am I ?
> An infant crying in the night :
> An infant crying for the light :
> And with no language but a cry."

In Poem cxxiv., stanza 5, he says,

> " Then was I as a child that cries,
> But, crying, knows his father near."

LV.

He pursues the awful theme, and asks whether the universal wish for restoration to life, does not spring from what is "likest God" in our own souls, a consciousness of immortality?

> " Are God and Nature then at strife ? "

for we find Nature, whilst careful in preserving the type of each species, utterly reckless of the separate members. We find too, that out of fifty seeds sown, only one perhaps germinates. He falters and falls down

> " Upon the great world's altar-stairs,
> That slope thro' darkness up to God ; "[a]

but still he stretches forth "lame hands of faith."

[a] In Pope's "Essay on Man," line 332, we read
"Looks through Nature up to Nature's God."

> " To what I feel is Lord of all,
> And faintly trust the larger hope "—

the hope of a final restitution of all things.

LVI.

He said that Nature preserved each type; but no, some species are already extinct. In geological strata, we find the fossil remains of creatures that no longer exist. Why then may not man,

> " who seem'd so fair,
> Such splendid purpose in his eyes,"

also perish, and have his dust blown about the desert,

> " Or seal'd within the iron hills ? "

If he be "no more"—if there be nothing beyond this life for him— then is man but a monster, a dream, a discord—"dragons of the prime," the Ichthyosauri that lived in the slime of chaos, were his betters!

> " O life as futile, then, as frail !
>   O for thy voice to soothe and bless ! [a]
>   What hope of answer or redress ?
> Behind the veil, behind the veil."

LVII.

" Peace, come away," may possibly be addressed to his sister, whom he now calls away from the sad subject which his earthly song had treated.

He says his companion's cheeks are pale, so it is time that they should turn to other things, though in doing so, he must leave half his own life behind. His "friend is richly shrined ;" but what will become of himself ? "I shall pass ; my work will fail."

It is difficult to trace in these words the Poet's exact meaning. Does he mean that he shall die without worthily commemorating his

---

[a] " But O for the touch of a vanish'd hand,
    And the sound of a voice that is still."

friend ? At any rate, so long as he lives will the tolling of Hallam's passing bell[a] be in his ears; and the strokes on the bell, "Ave" and "Adieu," hail and farewell, are like the notes of perpetual separation. They seem to be parted "for ever-more."[b]   He is in the lowest depth of woe.

LVIII.

It has been thought that there might have been an interval after the composition of the previous Poem ; and that the author resumed his task in a more hopeful state of mind.

He now compares the words of his late farewell to the echoes of dropping water in burial vaults, and he says that other hearts besides his own were affected by his lamentation.

---

a The term "toll" is correct—
> "When we lament a departed soul
> We toll."

b *Dixitque novissima verba*, Æ. iv., 650.

Urania reproaches him for thus distributing a fruitless grief amongst those who had shared his sense of loss; and, exhorting him to wait with patience for a more resigned feeling, she assures him that it will come to his great relief—

> "Abide a little longer here,
> And thou shalt take a nobler leave"—

be able to speak with more hope of meeting again.

LIX.

He invites Sorrow to live with him as a wife, always and constant, not as a casual mistress: being his "bosom-friend and half of life," even as it were Hallam himself.

Sorrow must remain his centred passion which cannot move; nevertheless it will not always be gloomy: but rather allow occasional playfulness, so that it would not be commonly known that he had a life-long affliction.[a]

LX.

He cannot dismiss the memory of his loss, and calls Hallam "a soul of nobler tone," superior to himself, who is feeling "like some poor girl" that has fixed her affections on a man of higher rank than her own. She compares her state with his, and sighs over her own inferior ˏcircumstances, and repines at her humbler lot. The neighbours jeer at her disappointment, and she says

> "How vain am I !
> How should he love a thing so low ? "

LXI.

If Hallam, in the intermediate state, be exchanging replies with the great intellects there assembled from all

[a] There is often great charm in the cheerfulness of those who we know have suffered.

time,—" the spirits of just men made perfect "—how dwarfed and insignificant must seem any intercourse with his friend still left here—

" How blanch'd with darkness must I grow ! "

This figure of speech will be taken from the blanching of vegetables in the dark. Still, he would have him turn to

" the doubtful shore,
Where thy first form was made a man ; "

that is, to this world, distinguishing it from that " second state sublime," into which Hallam had been admitted; for not even there can more affection be found, than I conceived and yet cherish :

" I loved thee, Spirit, and love, nor can
The soul of Shakespeare love thee more."

This is all that even Shakespeare can do, if he and thou be now compeers.

LXII.

If looking down on his affection
makes his friend ashamed, then let
their friendship be to him but as an
idle tale or legend of the past. And
Hallam may feel as one might, who
having once had a low attachment,
did afterwards wed an equal mind.[a]

The first love then either wholly
dies out, or

> " Is matter for a flying smile "—

a subject for ridicule.

LXIII.

Still, if I can pity an overdriven
horse, or love my dog, without robbing
heaven of its dues of reverence, when
these animals are as much below me
as I am thy inferior; why mayst not
thou "watch me, where I weep," from
thy circuits of higher heights and
deeper depths than mine?

[a] "Thou, as one that once declined," recalls in Hamlet,
Act I., s. 5, "To decline upon a wretch, whose natural
gifts were poor to those of mine."

5

LXIV.

He asks whether Hallam is looking back on this life,

"As some divinely gifted man,"

who has burst through all the adverse circumstances of his humble birth, by genius and labour ; making

"by force his merit known,
And lives to clutch the golden keys,
To mould a mighty state's decrees,
And shape the whisper of the throne ;"

as Lord Beaconsfield has done. Does not such a hero in his elevation,

"When all his active powers are still,"

sometimes feel tender memories of the scenes of his early life—

"The limit of his narrower fate "—

when "he play'd at counsellors and kings" with some lad long ago left behind in his native obscurity ; and

who now resting on his plough,
musingly asks,

"Does my old friend remember me ?"

LXV.

He clings to the memory of Hallam,
yet would resign himself to his loss—

"Sweet soul, do with me as thou wilt."

All that he can resolve is, to cherish
every grain of love ; and in doing so,
there springs up the "happy thought,"
that if his own nature has been
elevated by intercourse with Hallam,
why may not a like result have been
reflected from himself on his friend ?

"Since we deserved the name of friends,
    And thine effect so lives in me,
    A part of mine may live in thee,
And move thee on to noble ends."

LXVI.

He accounts for his cheerfulness to
some one, who had wondered that

being so far diseased in heart he could ever be gay.

He says that his own grief has made him feel kindly towards others; and that he is like a blind man, who though needing a hand to lead him, can still jest with his friends, take children on his knee and play with them, and dream of the sky he can no longer see:

> " His inner day can never die,
> His night of loss is always there."

LXVII.

He pictures in his mind, as he lies in bed, how the moonlight that fills his chamber is passing its " silver flame " across the marble tablet in Clevedon Church,[a] which is inscribed

a Clevedon Church is quaint and picturesque in appearance, but not architecturally beautiful. It is an irregular structure, which has evidently been added to at various times, the chancel being the original fisherman's church, and it has a solid square tower. Within the sanctuary is the Hallam vault, on which the organ now stands. Two cliffs, rounded and grass-grown, that rise on either side, seem to guard and shelter it, with its surrounding church-yard that holds the quiet dead.

to the memory of Hallam. The tablet is not in the chancel of the church, as described in the earlier editions of this Poem, but on the west wall of the south transept; and "the letters of thy name," and "the number of thy years," are thus most affectingly recorded:

"TO THE MEMORY OF
ARTHUR HENRY HALLAM,
OF TRINITY COLLEGE, CAMBRIDGE, B.A.,
ELDEST SON OF HENRY HALLAM, ESQUIRE,
AND OF JULIA MARIA, HIS WIFE,
DAUGHTER OF SIR ABRAHAM ELTON, BART.,
OF CLEVEDON COURT,
WHO WAS SNATCHED AWAY BY SUDDEN DEATH,
AT VIENNA, ON SEPTEMBER 15TH, 1833,
IN THE 23RD YEAR OF HIS AGE.
AND NOW, IN THIS OBSCURE AND SOLITARY
CHURCH,
REPOSE THE MORTAL REMAINS OF
ONE TOO EARLY LOST FOR PUBLIC FAME,
BUT ALREADY CONSPICUOUS AMONG HIS
CONTEMPORARIES
FOR THE BRIGHTNESS OF HIS GENIUS,
THE DEPTH OF HIS UNDERSTANDING,
THE NOBLENESS OF HIS DISPOSITION,
THE FERVOUR OF HIS PIETY,
AND THE PURITY OF HIS LIFE.

> *Vale dulcissime,*
> *vale dilectissime, desideratissime,*
> *requiescas in pace.*
> *Pater ac mater hic posthac requiescamus tecum,*
> *usque ad tubam."* [a]

When the moonlight dies he falls asleep, "closing eaves of wearied eyes;" and awakens to know how the grey break of day is drawn from "coast to coast," across the Severn,

> " And in the dark church like a ghost
> Thy tablet glimmers to the dawn."

LXVIII.

A succession of dreams now occur. When at night he presses "the down"

[a] There are other tablets in this church, which contain affecting memorials of the Hallam family. The Historian's own death is recorded as having taken place on 21st January, 1859. Mrs. Hallam died 28th April, 1840. Their son Henry Fitzmaurice died at Sienna, 25th October, 1850, aged 26; and he is said, by one who knew him, to have had all the charm and talent of Arthur. On 13th June, 1837, in her 21st year, Eleanor Hallam was suddenly called away, and was buried in the vault where her brother, Arthur, had been laid.

It was after this sad bereavement, that Mr. and Mrs. Hallam made a brief sojourn at Sevenoaks, then unspotted by villas, where they lived in strict retirement. Mr. Hallam only associated with Sir John Bayley, the retired judge, who was a kind friend of my own youth. I see the sorrowing couple at church in garments of the deepest mourning ; and the fine brow of Mr. Hallam resting on his hand, as he stood during the service in pensive devotion.—A.G.

of his pillow, sleep, " Death's twin-brother,"a "times my breath "—takes possession of him.   But, though so closely related to Death, sleep cannot make him dream of Hallam "as dead." He again walks with him, as he did before he was left "forlorn ;" and all nature is bright around them.

But, looking at his friend, he discovers "a trouble in thine eye "—an expression of sadness, which his dream will not account for.   The light of day reveals the truth.   He awakes, and perceives that his own grief, the trouble of his youth, had transferred itself to the image he saw in his dream.

LXIX.

He dreams again, and nature seems to have become distorted, and will not answer to the seasons.   Smoke and

a *Consanguineus leti sopor.*   Æn. vi., 278.

frost fill the streets, and hawkers chatter trifles at the doors.

He wanders into a wood, and finds only "thorny boughs." Of these he forms a crown, which he places on his head. For wearing this, he is scoffed at and derided; but an angel comes and touches it into leaf, and speaks words of comfort, "hard to understand," being the language of a higher world.

The occurences in this dream seem to have been suggested by the indignities offered to our Lord before His crucifixion.

LXX.

The confusion of nightmare succeeds, with hideous imagery; till all at once the horrid shapes disperse, and his nerves are composed by a pleasanter vision:

> " I hear a wizard music roll,
> And thro' a lattice on the soul
> Looks thy fair face and makes it still."

LXXI.

Sleep, from its capturing power over the brain, is called "kinsman to death and trance and madness;" and is here acknowledged as affording

"A night-long Present of the Past,"

by reviving in a dream the tour they had made together "thro' summer France."

The Poet asks that, if sleep has "such credit with the soul," as to produce this temporary illusion; it may be farther extended by giving him a stronger opiate, so as to make his pleasure complete, in prolonging this renewal of their pedestrian tour, and reviving other cherished associations.

This reference to their foreign excursion recalls the charming verses, "In the Valley of Cauteretz," which evidently relate to their being together during this happy holiday :

" All along the valley, stream that flashest white,
Deepening thy voice with the deepening of the
    night,
All along the valley, where thy waters flow,
I walk'd with one I loved two-and-thirty years
    ago.
All along the valley, while I walk'd to-day,
The two-and-thirty years were a mist that rolls
    away ;
For all along the valley, down thy rocky bed,
Thy living voice to me was as the voice of the
    dead,
And all along the valley, by rock and cave and
    tree,
The voice of the dead was a living voice to me."

LXXII.

The dreams are over, and he addresses the anniversary of Hallam's death, which took place on the 15th September, 1833—the day having just dawned with stormy accompaniments. The poplar tree is blown white, through having its leaves reversed by the wind ; and the window-pane streams with rain. It is a day on which his " crown'd estate," his life's happiness, began to fail; and that the rose is weighed down by rain, and the daisy closes " her crimson fringes," [a] are effects quite in harmony with his feelings.

But, if the day had opened with no wind, and the sun had chequered the hill sides with light and shadow; it would still have looked

"As wan, as chill, as wild as now."

It is a disastrous "day, mark'd as with some hideous crime," he can therefore only say, "hide thy shame beneath the ground," in sunset, when the recalling anniversary will be past.

We are reminded of Job's imprecation on his own birthday—"Let the day perish on which I was born."

[a] The foot of "Maud" opened these fringes by treading on the daisies. "Her feet have touch'd the meadows, and left the daisies rosy."

LXXIII.

He says there are so many worlds, and so much to be done in them—since so little has already been accomplished—that he thinks Hallam may have been needed elsewhere. The earthly career of usefulness and distinction is over, but he finds no fault, piously submitting—

> " For nothing is that errs from law ;"

all is overruled. We pass away, and what survives of human deeds ?

> " It rests with God."

The hollow ghost of Hallam's reputation may wholly fade here ; but his exulting soul carries away unexpended powers for higher purposes,

> " And self-infolds the large results
> Of force that would have forged a name,"

had he been permitted to live.

LXXIV.

This Poem will certainly not bear a literal interpretation. We cannot suppose that the writer ever looked on the face of his friend after death; for nearly four months had elapsed before the body reached England.

What he *saw*, therefore, was "with the mind's eye." And as Death often brings out a likeness, which was never before recognised; so, contemplating the character of the departed, he sees

> " Thy likeness to the wise below,
> Thy kindred with the great of old."

I can perceive worth in thee equal to theirs!

The last stanza is mystical; the darkness of death hides much; what he can see he cannot or will not explain: enough, that thou hast made even this darkness of death beautiful by thy presence.

LXXV.

The Poet leaves the praises of his friend unexpressed, because no words can duly convey them; and the greatness thus unrecorded must be guessed, by the measure of the survivor's grief. Indeed, he does not care

> " in these fading days
> To raise a cry that lasts not long,
> And round thee with the breeze of song,
> To stir a little dust[a] of praise."

The world only applauds accomplished success, and does not care for what might have been done, had opportunity been given. It is therefore sufficient that silence should guard Hallam's fame here; because

[a] In "The Two Voices," Tennyson says,

> " I know that age to age succeeds,
> Blowing a noise of tongues and deeds,
> A *dust* of systems and of creeds."

And again, in "The Vision of Sin,"

> " All the windy ways of men
> Are but *dust* that rises up,
> And is lightly laid again."

the writer is assured, that what he is elsewhere doing

" Is wrought with tumult of acclaim."

One cannot but feel that were it not for this immortal elegy, its subject would have been long since forgotten, like other promising youths who have died in their Spring.

LXXVI.

"Take wings of fancy," and imagine that you have the whole "starry heavens of space" revealed to one glance — " sharpen'd to a needle's end."a

"Take wings of foresight," and see in the future how thy best poems are dumb, before a yew tree moulders; and though the song of the morning stars at the Creation may last, thy songs in fifty years will have become

a Shakespeare says,—"Till the diminution of space had pointed him sharp as my needle."—*Cymbeline*, Act i., s. 4.

vain; and have ceased to be known by the time when the oak tree has withered into a hollow ruin.

LXXVII.

" What hope is here for modern rhyme?"

Looking at what has already happened,

" These mortal lullabies of pain,"

may bind a book, or line a box, or be used by some girl for curl papers; or before a century has passed, they may be found on a stall, telling of

" A grief—then changed to something else,
Sung by a long forgotten mind."

Nevertheless, these considerations shall not deter the Poet—

" But what of that?   My darken'd ways
Shall ring with music all the same;
To breathe my loss is more than fame,
To utter love more sweet than praise."

LXXVIII.

Another Christmas Eve arrives, with snow and calm frosty weather. Though, as of old, they had games, and *tableaux vivants*, and dance, and song, and " hoodman-blind "[a]—blindman's buff—yet in spite of these recreations,

> " over all things brooding slept
> The quiet sense of something lost."

There were no visible signs of distress—no tears, or outward mourning. Could regret then have died out ?

> " No—mixt with all this mystic frame,
> Her deep relations are the same,
> But with long use her tears are dry."

LXXIX.

> " More than my brothers are to me "—

he had used this expression in the last stanza of Poem ix., and in repeating

---

[a] This term is Shakespearean,
> "What devil was't
> That thus hath cozen'd you at hoodman-blind."
> *Hamlet*, Act iii, s. 4.

6

it he would apologise to his brother, Charles Tennyson, we may presume.

"Let not this vex thee, noble heart!"

for thou art holding "the costliest love in fee," even a wife's affection —we may again suppose.

The Rev. Charles Tennyson married an heiress, and changed his name to Turner, and was vicar of Grasby, in Lincolnshire. At his recent death, the Poet Laureate became his heir, and the name and property are said to have been assumed by the younger of his two sons. It would indeed have been sacrilege to have merged the name of Tennyson.

Though the two brothers had now each their separate and supreme idols, they were still "one in kind," saw the same scenes in childhood, prayed at one mother's knee, learned from one book, when their flaxen hair was still undarkened.

And now, as we have our respective objects of higher love, "my wealth resembles thine." But Hallam

> " was rich where I was poor,
> And he supplied my want the more
> As his unlikeness fitted mine."

LXXX.

If any vague wish visits the Poet, that he had himself been the first to be removed by Death (when the dust would have dropt on "tearless eyes," which, as it is, have now so sorely wept over Hallam's departure); then the grief of the survivor would have been

> " as deep as life or thought,
> But stay'd in peace with God and man;"

because Hallam would have found comfort in pious resignation.

So he minutely ponders over this holy submission, and invokes contentment from the contemplation—

> " Unused example from the grave
> Reach out dead hands to comfort me."

LXXXI.

If, whilst Hallam was with him, it could be said that love had its full complement and satisfaction, and could not range beyond ; still he torments himself with "this haunting whisper,"

> " More years had made me love thee more."

My attachment would have expanded with the enlargement of his powers.

> " But Death returns an answer sweet :
> My sudden frost was sudden gain "—

The change in death instantly exalted its victim ;

> " And gave all ripeness to the grain,
> It might have drawn from after-heat."

A sudden frost will ripen grain or fruit, but will not impart the flavour to fruit which the sun gives.

It may be remarked that the Poet often personifies " sorrow," " death," &c., as if Hallam himself were addressed.

LXXXII.

A fine burst of Faith in the future. He does not reproach Death for any corruption by it " on form or face." No decay of the flesh can shake his trust. in the survival of the soul. " Eternal process " is ever " moving on ;" the Spirit walks through a succession of states of being ; and the body dropt here is but a case, the " ruin'd crysalis of one " state left behind.[a]

Nor does he find fault with Death for taking " virtue out of earth :" he knows that it will be transplanted elsewhere to greater profit.

[a] In " The Two Voices " we find the idea that man may pass "from state to state," and forget the one he leaves behind :

> " As old mythologies relate,
> Some draught of Lethe might await
> The slipping thro' from state to state."

What he is angry with Death for is, their separation—

> " He put our lives so far apart
> We cannot hear each other speak."

This Poem expresses a comforting belief in progress and advancement hereafter.

LXXXIII.

He reproaches the New Year for "delaying long." Its advent would cheer him, bringing the light and sweetness of spring—for

> " Can trouble live with April days,
> Or sadness in the summer moons ? "

He would have the New Year bring all its customary flowers—

> " Deep tulips dash'd with fiery dew,
> Laburnums, dropping wells of fire "—

a sight of these would set free the sorrow in his blood,

> " And flood a fresher throat with song."

LXXXIV.

This Poem is a very charming conception of what their lives might domestically have been, if Hallam had been spared. The picture is almost too beautiful: detailing more than life ever allows—and there came the crushing sorrow.

Engaged in marriage to the Poet's sister,[a] death intervened—

> " that remorseless iron hour
> Made cypress of her orange flower,
> Despair of Hope, and earth of thee."

It is remarkable how the imagination of the Poet glows over the tender scenes of home affection, and the great results which he presumes were arrested by the removal of his friend, who he had hoped would have attained " to reverence and the silver

[a] Miss Emily Tennyson eventually married a naval officer, Captain Jesse.

hair" in company with himself—and then, in their full old age,

> " He that died in Holy Land
> Would reach us out the shining hand,
> And take us as a single soul."

The mere thought of this forbidden consummation of their friendship shocks him; it revives the old bitterness of sorrow, and stops

> " The low beginnings of content."[a]

LXXXV.

The first stanza merely repeats the sentiment expressed in Poem xxvii., that the deepest grief has only more

---

a In this Poem occurs the line
> " Arrive at last the blessed goal."

" Arrive " is thus made an active verb : but there are good authorities for this use, which has the meaning of " attain," or " reach."

> " But ere we could arrive the point proposed,
> Cæsar cried, Help me, Cassius, or I sink."
>> *Julius Cæsar*, Act i., s. 2.

> " I mean, my lords, those powers that the queen
> Hath raised in Gallia have arrived our coast."
>> 3 *Henry VI.*, Act v., s. 3.

> " Over the vast abrupt, ere he arrive
> The happy isle."
>> *Paradise Lost*, B. II., l. 409.

fully convinced him, that to have loved and lost is better than never to have loved.

It must be his once affianced sister, "true in word and tried in deed," who asks how he is affected—if his faith be still firm, and he has still room in his heart for love ? He answers, that all was well with him, until that fatal "message" came that

"God's finger touch'd him, and he slept."

He then recounts what he thinks may have occurred to his friend, when translated through various stages of spiritual being; and he repeats his sorrowful regrets for his loss. But "I woo your love," he seems to say to his sister, for he holds it wrong

"to mourn for any over much:"

still, so deep is his attachment to Hallam, that he calls himself

> " the divided half of such
> A friendship as had master'd Time ; "

their intimacy would be eternal ; and he imagines some sort of intercourse still carried on betwixt them, which he describes in language that has much of the spirit and character of Dante.

He then seems to turn again to his sister, and says,

> " If not so fresh, with love as true,
> I, clasping brother-hands, aver
> I could not, if I would, transfer
> The whole I felt for him to you."

A later stanza must, I think, refer to the lady who became Mrs. Tennyson :

> " My heart, tho' widow'd, may not rest
> Quite in the love of what is gone,
> But seeks to beat in time with one
> That warms another living breast."

The concluding stanza offers the primrose of autumn to the sister, whilst that of spring must be reserved for his lost friend.

LXXXVI.

He asks the ambrosial air of
evening, which is so "sweet after
showers," and is "slowly breathing
bare the round of space," clearing the
sky of clouds, and "shadowing" the
divided stream by raising ripples on
its surface, to fan the fever from his
cheek, till Doubt and Death can no
longer enchain his fancy, but will let
it fly to the rising star, in which

"A hundred spirits whisper, ' Peace.'"

LXXXVII.

He revisits Cambridge, the chief
scene of past intimacy with Hallam,
and roams about the different colleges.
The expression "high-built organ,"
probably alludes to the organ being
here, as in some cathedrals, reared
above the screen which separates the
chapel from the ante-chapel.

"The prophets blazon'd on the panes,"

refer to the stained glass windows, and more particularly to those, perhaps, in King's College chapel. The scenery at the back of the colleges is vividly recalled.

He stops at the door of Hallam's old room, now occupied by a noisy wine party. It was there that his friend used to achieve such controversial triumphs—ever as the master-bowman hitting the mark in argument, when

"we saw
The God within him light his face,"

like the martyr Stephen's ;

"And over those ethereal eyes
The bar of Michael Angelo "—

whose brow was straight and prominent —the sign of intellectual power.

LXXXVIII.

He asks the "wild bird," probably

the nightingale, whose liquid song brings a sense of Eden back again, to define the feelings of the heart, its emotions and passions. In the "budded quicks" of Spring the bird is happy; in the "darkening leaf," amid the shadowing foliage, though its happiness be gone, its grieving heart can still cherish "a secret joy." The notes of the nightingale are supposed to be both sorrowful and joyous.

Even so, the Poet cannot wholly govern his own muse; for, when he would sing of woe,

> "The glory of the sum of things,"

the grandeur of life's experience, will sometimes rule the chords.

LXXXIX.

This Poem is like a picture by Watteau of a summer holiday in the garden or the woods.

He recalls the lawn of Somersby Rectory, with the trees that shade it, and Hallam as being present on one of his repeated visits. He has come down from his law readings in the Temple,

"The dust and din and steam of town;"

and now, in a golden afternoon, sees

"The landscape winking thro' the heat,"

as he lies and reads Dante, or Tasso, aloud to his companions; until later on, when some lady of the group would bring her harp, and fling

"A ballad to the brightening moon."

Or the family party may have strayed further away, for a pic-nic in the woods; and are there discussing the respective merits of town and country.

They are described as returning home,

> " Before the crimson-circled star
> Had fall'n into her father's grave,"

that is, before the planet Venus had sunk into the sea. The mutilated remains of Uranus were cast into the sea, from which the goddess Venus was said to have been born.

The evening sounds are very charming—

> " The milk that bubbled in the pail,
> And buzzings of the honied hours,"

when the bees were gathering their last stores of the day. Tender recollections of the past !

XC.

He is indignant at the idea that if the dead came back to life again, they would not be welcome; and declares that whoever suggested this, could never have tasted the highest love. Nevertheless, if the father did return to life, he would probably find his wife remarried, and his son unwilling to give up the estate. Even if matters were not so bad as this, still

> " the yet-loved sire would make
> Confusion worse than death, and shake
> The pillars of domestic peace."[a]

Though all this may be true,

> " I find not yet one lonely thought
> That cries against my wish for thee."

XCI.

When the larch is in flower, and the thrush " rarely pipes " — exquisitely sings ; and " the sea-blue bird of March,"[b] the king-fisher, " flits by ; "

[a] In the Lotus Eaters," we read
> " all hath suffered change ;
> For surely now our household hearths are cold :
> Our sons inherit us : our looks are strange :
> And we should come like ghosts to trouble joy."

[b] The kingfisher is here meant, which, like other birds, puts on its best plumage in early spring—see " Locksley Hall "—
> " In the spring a fuller crimson comes upon the robin's breast ;
> In the spring the wanton lapwing gets himself another crest ;
> In the spring a livelier iris changes on the burnished dove."

come, my friend, in thy spirit-form, with thy brow wearing the tokens of what thou hast become. Come to me also in the summer-time, when roses bloom and the wheat ripples in the wind. Don't come at night, but whilst the sunbeam is warm, that I may see thee,

> " beauteous in thine after form,
> And like a finer light in light."

XCII.

If a vision revealed Hallam in bodily presence as of old, he would doubt its reality, and ascribe it to "the canker of the brain." If the apparition spoke of the past, he would still call it only "a wind of memory" in himself. Even if it promised what afterwards came true, he would account it to be merely a presentiment—

7

> " such refraction of events
> As often rises ere they rise."[a]

XCIII.

"I shall not see thee;" for he doubts, though he dares not positively speak, whether a spirit does ever return to this world—at least visibly—so as to be recognised. But he will dare to ask that where "the nerve of sense" is not concerned—that is, where neither sight nor touch are needed—"Spirit to Spirit, Ghost to Ghost" may come, so that

> " My Ghost may feel that thine is near."

XCIV.

To be fit and capable of a spiritual visitation from the dead, you must be "pure in heart and sound in head."

---

[a] Campbell says, " Coming events cast their shadows before." The sun, by refraction, still appears in full size above the horizon, after it has really sunk below it ; and reappears in full, when only just the upper edge has reached the horizon.

There will be no answer to your invocation, unless you can say that your "spirit is at peace with all," as they can who are already in "their golden day" in Paradise. The mind and memory and conscience must be calm and still ; for

> " when the heart is full of din,
> And doubt beside the portal waits,"

the departed spirits

> " can but listen at the gates,
> And hear the household jar within."

This fitness for apprehending any communications from the next world, well describes the condition requisite for intercourse with God Himself.

XCV.

Here comes another family scene at Somersby.[a]

---

a Somersby has been described to me by a friend who has visited the spot, as being utterly secluded from the " madding crowd "—the most rural retirement that the most

It may be observed here that Dr. Tennyson, the Poet's father, had died in 1831, but his family occupied the Rectory for several years afterwards, as the new Incumbent was non-resident.

The family party are at tea on the lawn in the calm summer evening. No wind makes the tapers flare, no cricket chirrs, only the running brook is heard at a distance, whilst the urn flutters on the table.   The bats,

> "with ermine capes
> And woolly breasts and beaded eyes,"

wheel about in the dusk; and those

agricultural county can show. I find the population was recorded in 1835, when the family still resided there, as being sixty-one, whilst the church accommodation was for sixty. Small, however, as both church and parish were, and still are, the Rectory is a roomy family house, with its back to the road, on which there can be but little traffic, and it fronts a very extensive stretch of country, on which you enter by a steep slope of ground. There are no striking features in this expanse of soft undulations, but you feel a consciousness that the sea is not far off, and that the scenery is well adapted for fine cloud and sunset effects. The air was felt to have a bracing tone, and the several equally small churches around, told of thin populations, and a general condition of rustic simplicity and peace.

assembled sing old songs, which are heard as far as where the cows are lying under the branching trees.

So passed the evening until all have retired to rest, and the Poet is alone, when he takes out Hallam's last-written letters—

> "those fall'n leaves which kept their green,
> The noble letters of the dead."

He reads them afresh, to renew a sense of their bygone intimacy:

> "So word by word, and line by line,
>   The dead man touch'd me from the past,
>   And all at once it seem'd at last
> The living soul was flash'd on mine."

The Poet's mind struggles on "empyreal heights of thought" in incorporeal ecstacy—a sort of trance inexplicable—which lasts till dawn, when

> "East and West, without a breath,
>   Mixt their dim lights, like life and death,
> To broaden into boundless day."

XCVI.

He reproves the young lady, who, whilst tender over killing a fly, does not hesitate to call the harass of religious doubt "Devil-born."

The Poet says, "one indeed I knew"—who, it may be presumed, was Hallam—and

> "He faced the spectres of the mind
> And laid them."
> "Perplext in faith, but pure in deeds,
> At last he beat his music out,"

and found the serenity of faith.

> "There lives more faith in honest doubt,
> Believe me, than in half the creeds."

Unquestioning faith is not the quali-fication for its champion. True faith is the result of conflict—"the victory that overcometh the world."

God made and lives in both light and darkness; and is present in the trouble of doubt, as well as in the comfort of belief. The Israelites were making idols, when God's presence in the cloud was manifested by the trumpet. They doubted in the midst of sensible proof of the Divine presence.

The questionings of a speculative mind ought to be tenderly dealt with, not harshly denounced.

XCVII.

This Poem is highly mystical.

"My love has talk'd with rocks and trees."

His own affection for Hallam seems to personate the object of his attachment, and "sees himself in all he sees." Just as the giant spectre, sometimes seen "on misty mountain-ground," is no more than a vast shadow of the spectator himself.

The Poem proceeds more intelligibly, by drawing a comparison which typifies his own humble relation to his exalted friend. He imagines some meek-hearted and affectionate wife loving and revering a husband, whose high intellect and pursuits exclude her from any real companionship.

But she treasures any little memorials of their early devotion, and feeling that he is

> " great and wise,
> She dwells on him with faithful eyes,
> 'I cannot understand : I love.'"

XCVIII.

"You leave us." Some one is going on the very route which the friends had traversed together, and will reach "that City," Vienna, where Hallam died. All its splendour is to the Poet,

> " No livelier than the wisp ᵃ that gleams
> On Lethe in the eyes of Death;"

ᵃ *Ignis fatuus*—"Will o' the Wisp."

so great is his aversion to the place, on account of the loss he had sustained there; and he charges it with all manner of ill.

But Hallam had given him a very different description; saying that in no other metropolis—"mother town" —had he seen such stately carriages of the rich pass to and fro; and such a contented crowd enjoying themselves with dance and song, amidst a display of coloured fireworks.

XCIX.

This Poem is an address to the recurring anniversary of Hallam's death, which had before been commemorated in Poem lxxii—

"Day when I lost the flower of men."

The early signs of Autumn are very sweetly described, in personifying a day that will remind many of births and bridals, but still more of deaths; and wherever the sorrowing survivors may reside, they are on this day "kindred souls" with himself—though they be utter strangers—

"They know me not, but mourn with me."

This applies to all

"Betwixt the slumber of the poles"—

from one end of the world to the other.

The poles of the earth are the ends of the axis on which the world revolves. These never move, but "slumber."

C.

Rising from his night's rest, shortly before quitting the old home, and looking over the familiar landscape, which his friend had known so well; there is not a feature but recalls some gracious memory of Hallam's presence.

The various objects in the surrounding country are enumerated, and present a beautiful rural picture to the mind ; and he says,

> " But each has pleased a kindred eye,
> And each reflects a kindlier day ;
> And, leaving these, to pass away,
> I think once more he seems to die."

To take leave of them is to renew the more bitter separation.

In recent editions, this Poem commences " I climb the hill," instead of " I wake, I rise."

CI.

A sad reflection comes over him at the thought of bidding farewell to Somersby.

Unwatched and unloved will the flowers in the garden bloom with their fragrance, although the family be gone : and the trees will put forth, and afterwards shed their foliage. The rose-carnation, too, will

> "feed
> With summer-spice the humming air,"

in which the bees are busy.
Uncared for, the brook will babble

> "At noon, or when the lesser wain [a]
> Is twisting round the polar star;"—

also when the sailing moon's reflection in the water becomes broken into silver arrows.[b]
All this will go on, until garden and wild become familiar to the succeeding stranger:

> "And year by year our memory fades
> From all the circle of the hills."

[a] That is, the *ursa minor*, or little bear, which is a small constellation that contains the pole star, and never sets in our latitude.

[b] This is a favourite figure. In Poem xlix., stanza 1, we read,

> "Like light in many a shiver'd lance
> That breaks about the dappled pool."

Future generations will nevertheless visit Somersby, with something of the reverence that still attracts the stranger to Stratford-on-Avon.

CII.

> " We leave the well-beloved place
>   Where first we gazed upon the sky."

The mother, and the members of her family, quit the Rectory, and seek a new home.

But, "ere we go," the Poet walks in the garden, and seems to be in the company of two spirits, who

> " Contend for loving masterdom."

These are Dr. Tennyson and Arthur Hallam. The former, being his father, pleads, as a claim for the son's best affection, that

> " here thy boyhood sung
> Long since its matin song."

In 1827, the two brothers, Alfred and

Charles Tennyson, published a joint volume of Poems; and the shade of the father would now make the old home dear and valued by this reminiscence.

The rival spirit urges

> "yea, but here
> Thy feet have stray'd in after hours
> With thy lost friend among the bowers,
> And this hath made them trebly dear."

Through half the day each prefers his separate appeal by endearing circumstance; but the contest affords no superiority to either; and, as the Poet turns away from the illusion,

> "They mix in one another's arms
> To one pure image of regret."

This picture is very beautiful.

CIII.

A dream is described,

> "Which left my after-morn content;"

it imparted comfort.

The Poet seemed to be in a hall, where maidens were singing before a veiled statue—

> " known to me,
> The shape of him I loved."

A dove flies in and summons him to the sea, where, together with his female companions, he enters a boat. As the boat glides away with them, they all seem to expand into greater size and strength; and a vast ship meets them, on the deck of which, in giant proportions, stands " the man we loved."

The maidens weep, as they fear being left behind; but all enter the ship, and

> " We steer'd her toward a crimson cloud
> That land-like slept along the deep."

I can only surmise that this vision may possibly symbolize a future reunion, when the Poet and his sisters will meet Hallam on the golden shore.

CIV.

Christmastide again ; and he hears the bells from

"A single church below the hill ; "

this is at the place to which the family have moved. It is a fresh and strange locality, and the bells sound like strangers' voices, recalling nothing of his previous life ; no memory can stray in the surrounding scenery ;

"But all is new unhallow'd ground."

CV.[a]

It is Christmas Eve, but the holly outside their new home shall stand ungathered. He deprecates repeating their old observances of this season

a "This holly by the cottage-eave,
     To-night, ungather'd, shall it stand."
Changed in later editions to
    "To-night ungather'd let us leave
      This laurel, let this holly stand."

in a new place.   He thinks of his father's grave "under other snows" than those he looks on; and how the violet will blow there, "but we are gone."

What was done in the old home cannot be repeated in the new habitation,

> " For change of place, like growth of time,
> Has broke the bond of dying use." [a]

He would have this Christmas Eve kept with reverent solemnity; no joyous forms retained, from which the spirit has gone; no music, dance, or motion,

> " save alone
> What lightens in the lucid east
> Of rising worlds by yonder wood."

This must refer to the rising sun, with the planets that move round it, and

[a] " Use and Wont,
Old sisters of a day gone by.
They too will die."—Poem xxix.

are considered to be "worlds." Let these run out their

"measured arcs, and lead
The closing cycle rich in good;"

bringing Christ's second advent.

CVI.

The old year is rung out by "wild bells to the wild sky;" and he would have these ring out all abuses and evils, and ring in all good, various blessings which he enumerates—

"Ring out the thousand wars of old,
Ring in the thousand years of peace."

the millenium; and, last of all,

"Ring in the Christ that is to be;"

God Himself again upon earth.

CVII.

"It is the day when he was born,"

the anniversary of Hallam's birth,

which took place in London, on 1st February, 1811.

One may suppose this Poem to have been written at night, because the description is of

> " A bitter day that early sank
> Behind a purple-frosty bank
> Of vapour, leaving night forlorn."

Indeed the time is determined by the poetry, for " yon hard crescent " shows that the moon was up when he was writing.

Ice making "daggers at the sharpen'd eaves" is a common sight. Such icicles may be sometimes seen a yard long, pendent from any eave or ledge.

" Brakes " may here mean " bracken;" "grides" may mean "grates;" and "iron horns" must be the dry hard forked boughs; but how distinguished from the " leafless ribs " of the wood, unless as descriptive of the forms of different trees in the wood, is difficult to understand.

> "the drifts that pass
> To darken on the rolling brine
> That breaks the coast,"

must allude to drifts of snow, which falling into water immediately blacken before they dissolve.

This birthday shall no more be kept as a day of mourning, but shall be joyously observed,

> "with festal cheer,
> With books and music, surely we
> Will drink to him whate'er he be,
> And sing the songs he loved to hear."

CVIII.

A noble resolution seems to be now formed, not to become morbid and misanthropic; and this feeling appears to sustain and animate the Poet throughout the remainder of his loving tribute.

He admits that "barren faith and vacant yearning" are profitless; although they may carry him in thought to the highest height of heaven, or to the deepest depth of Death. And, this being so, his upward glance only reveals

" mine own phantom chanting hymns ; "

or gazing below he sees

" The reflex of a human face."

His lost friend being, therefore, everywhere represented, he will try to extract wisdom from the sorrow which he cannot exclude; though this be not such wisdom as sleeps with Hallam.

CIX.

Hallam's character and accomplishments are recited. Richness of conversation, much imported from an intellectual home; with critical powers over all poetry. Keen and rapid thought displayed in logical argument.

Delighting in what is good, but not ascetic, and pure in life. Loving freedom, but without

"The blind hysterics of the Celt;"

and uniting manliness with female grace, which made him such a favourite with children.

If the survivor had seen and admired all these qualities, and not allowed such wisdom to make him wise, then shame be on him!

CX.

He recalls their former Cambridge discussions; and how Hallam's powers of conversation drew out

"The men of rathe and riper years;"

both the young and older. He gave confidence to the timid, the true-hearted held to him, and the deceitful were exposed,

"While I, thy dearest, sat apart"

watching these triumphs, and enjoying them as my own ; and though not possessing the tact, and art, and sweetness, and skill, yet I seemed to share in them, from the love and admiration which they inspired.

"And, born of love, the vague desire
That spurs an imitative will,"

rose in me, and made me wish to do likewise.

CXI.

"The churl in spirit" may be found in all ranks of society. Even the king, holding the golden ball of state, may be "at heart a clown."

The "coltish nature" will break out through all the disguises of fashion : but in Hallam

"God and Nature met in light,
And thus he bore without abuse
The grand old name of gentleman,
Defamed by every charlatan,
And soil'd with all ignoble use."

CXII.

"High wisdom," which judges *ex cathedrâ*, will condemn him for preferring "glorious insufficiencies" to "narrower perfectness."

He esteems high purposes after what is unattained, as exhibited in Hallam's shortened life; more than a complete fulfilment of lesser duties by the "lords of doom," who rule in our social system.

His friend was "some novel power," which

> "Sprang up for ever at a touch,
> And hope could never hope too much,
> In watching thee from hour to hour."

CXIII.

He persistently dwells on Hallam's capabilities. Sorrow may teach wisdom; but how much more sleeps with him, who would not only have guided the survivor, but served all public ends.

He thinks his friend might have become the leading statesman of the day—a pilot to weather the storm, when the greatest social agonies prevailed.

CXIV.

"Who loves not Knowledge"? He would have it pursued to its utmost limits; but in the keen searchings of the scientific there is this danger, that conclusions are apt to be accepted before they have been proved.

Science, too often,

> "leaps into the future chance,
> Submitting all things to desire.
> Half-grown as yet, a child, and vain "—

and therefore needing caution and restraint.

If separated from love and faith, she bursts

> " All barriers in her onward race
> For power."

Science is " second, not the first,"

> " For she is earthly of the mind,
> But Wisdom heavenly of the soul."

He would have the world wise and modest

> " like thee,
> Who grewest not alone in power
> And knowledge, but from hour to hour
> In reverence and in charity."

It may be remarked that, here and elsewhere, the Poet makes a distinction betwixt mind and soul. The former acquiring knowledge, which

> " is of things we see ; "

the latter by faith,

> " Believing where we cannot prove ; "

even those things which St. Paul says " are not seen and are eternal."

CXV.

Spring is described with its blossoming hedges and blowing violets.   The whole landscape changes in colour, with the warmer weather;

> " And drown'd in yonder living blue
> The lark becomes a sightless song." [a]

Who has not heard the lark, after it has become invisible in the heavens?
The migratory "birds that change their sky" [b] return and build their nests;

> " and my regret
> Becomes an April violet,
> And buds and blossoms like the rest."

He is cheered by the opening season.

CXVI.

Is it regret for buried time—grief for the friend whom he has lost—which makes him feel so tender and

a In *Measure for Measure*, Act iii., s. 1, we read,

"To be imprison'd in the viewless winds."

"Sightless" and "viewless" are alike used for "invisible."

b *Cœlum mutant, qui trans mare currunt.*
Hor. Ep. xi., 27.

susceptible of the influences of Spring?
Not wholly so : for "life re-orient out
of dust," the revival of vegetation
raises his spirits, and "heartens,"
strengthens his trust in that Power
which made the earth beautiful.

Nor is it altogether "regret" that
he feels; for the face and the voice of
his friend come back; and the voice
speaks of me and mine—his sister as
well as himself—and he is conscious
of

> " Less yearning for the friendship fled,
> Than some strong bond which is to be "—

reunion hereafter.

CXVII.

"O days and hours" [a]—he declares
their work to be the accumulation of
joy they will bring to that future
meeting, from which at present they
are detaining him.

[a] "Days and Hours" was the title of a volume of Poems
by Frederick Tennyson.

"Delight a hundredfold" will accrue from this postponement, the contribution of every grain of sand through the hour-glass, of "every span of shade" across the sundial, of every click in the watch, and each day's sun.

CXVIII.

A friend observes that this Poem is a remarkable exposition of the nebular hypothesis, as sanctioned by geologists.

Look at "this work of Time," its slow growth and effect; and don't believe that "human love and truth" dissolve and pass away, as being no more than "dying Nature's earth and lime," insensible and finite.

Rather trust that

> " the dead
> Are breathers of an ampler day
> For ever nobler ends."

If this solid earth came from elements dissolved by " fluent heat," and man was the last result; then he, who is now enduring fears and sorrows and the battering " shocks of doom," typifies " this work of time " on natural objects; for he must be, as they have been, in process of being moulded for a higher state. He is moving upward, " working out the beast," and letting " the ape and tiger die," while in his present probationary condition.

CXIX.

The work of resignation in the mourner's heart is here acknowledged. In Poem vii. he represents himself as standing, " like a guilty thing," at the door of the London house where they used to meet, and he was then all sad and comfortless.

But now he revisits the spot, at the same early hour, and his feelings have

changed and become reconciled and
hopeful.

> " I think of early days and thee,
> And bless thee, for thy lips are bland,
>   And bright the friendship of thine eye ;
>   And in my thoughts with scarce a sigh
> I take the pressure of thine hand."

CXX.

He exults in the victory of a
higher faith. We are not " magnetic
mockeries "—simply material " brain "
—" casts in clay "—to perish as soon
as the galvanic battery ceases to act,

> " not in vain,
> Like Paul with beasts, I fought with Death."

Let Science prove the contrary, even
that we only exist for this life, and I
won't stay here. And Science herself
would then be valueless, since she
had only taught us our nothingness.
Let " the wiser man " of the future

> " up from childhood shape
> His action like the greater ape,
> But I was born to other things."

This is spoken ironically, and is a strong protest against materialism and evolution. The gorilla is not our grandfather !

CXXI.

" Sad Hesper," the evening star, only rises to follow " the buried sun ; " but, in the. " dim and dimmer " light of late afternoon, it watches the conclusion of man's daily labours. The teams are loosened from the waggons, " the boat is drawn upon the shore," the house door is closed, " and life is darken'd in the brain " of the sleeper.

Phosphor, the morning star, sees the renewal of life ; the bird with its early song, the rising sun, the market boat again floating and voices calling to it from the shore, the village black-smith with his clinking hammer, and the team again harnessed and at work.

Hesper and Phosphor are simply the one planet Venus, which according to its position with the sun, becomes the morning or evening star.

So the Poet sings,

> " Sweet Hesper-Phosphor, double name
>   For what is one, the first, the last,
>   Thou, like my present and my past,
> Thy place is changed ; thou art the same."

Hallam has only been removed ; he is not altered into something else— " not lost, but gone before."

CXXII.

He seems to recall some former occasion, when in wild enquiry he had dared to question the great secrets of life and death—now and hereafter.

This may not refer to any special time, but to the general uneasiness of his feelings before submission had been attained; and he now says,

> " If thou wert with me, and the grave
> Divide us not, be with me now."

Let me again, "like an inconsiderate boy," "slip the thoughts of life and death," give free rein to a speculative imagination; for now, in a higher and better frame of mind, it will be that "every thought breaks out a rose"— a blossom of truth.

CXXIII.

The great changes on the earth's surface are bewildering, and hint that "nothing stands" and endures.

Where the tree now grows, and the long street is full of crowd and noise, there was once

"The stillness of the central sea."

The very hills and solid lands are no more than shadows, or

"Like clouds that shape themselves and go."

But our parting is not for ever,

"For tho' my lips may breathe adieu,
I cannot think the thing farewell."[a]

I am sure that we shall meet again.

CXXIV.

In this Poem we have a profound acknowledgement of the revealed Godhead in its triune manifestations, though not expressed in ecclesiastical formula :

"Our dearest faith; our ghastliest doubt;
He, They, One, All; within, without;
The Power in darkness whom we guess."

[a] What is the difference of meaning in the two words "adieu" and "farewell?" Byron says, in *Lara*,

"Farewell to life, but not adieu to thee."

This Power lives in our hearts. Eye hath not seen Him, nor is He to be found "in world or sun," or by dissection of what has lived, or by process of reasoning.

If ever his own faith faltered, and a voice said, "believe no more," the reproving witness was within himself.

> "A warmth within the breast would melt
> The freezing reason's colder part,
> And like a man in wrath the heart
> Stood up and answer'd, I have felt." [a]

Still he was

> "as a child that cries,
> But, crying, knows his father near." [b]

His own heart, which is the home of faith, testified to Divine truth, which

[a] "With the heart man believeth unto righteousness."
Romans x., 10.

[b] "But as I rav'd, and grew more fierce and wild
At every word,
Methought I heard one calling, *Child*,
And I reply'd, *My Lord*."

The Collar, G. Herbert.

"no man understands," but he accepts it as the one solution of what exists.

CXXV.

He admits that some "bitter notes" have sounded from his harp. But though his tongue may at times have seemed to speak with contradiction, Hope was nevertheless still alive to better things.

And if Love "play'd with gracious lies," suggested difficulties, this Love had only dared to do so

"Because he felt so fixed in truth."

Love sustained him when his song was "full of care;" and Love's signet marked it whenever it was "sweet and strong;" and he implores Love to abide with him till he joins his friend "on the mystic deeps," when his own electric brain no longer "keeps a thousand pulses dancing."

CXXVI.

Here is a noble testimony to the comfort and assurance which Love, when made our " Lord and King," can impart.

In the Poet's estimation, Love is the Charity of St. Paul ; believing, hoping, enduring, and never failing. Love brings us tidings of the dead. Love guards us in life, even in sleep. Through his influence we hear, as from a sentinel,

> " Who moves about from place to place,
> And whispers to the worlds of space,
> In the deep night, that all is well."

CXXVII.

Yes, "all is well, tho' faith and form be sunder'd" in temporary crises; that is, one must believe in ultimate good, even when the immediate circumstances are most adverse. The storm

will rage below on earth, before truth
and justice can be firmly established.

"The red fool-fury of the Seine"

probably refers to the Revolution of
1848, when both king and beggar, the
two poles of society, equally suffered.

Such convulsions will cease at last;
there is calm beyond; and, even
whilst they last,

"thou, dear spirit, happy star,
O'erlook'st the tumult from afar,
And smilest, knowing all is well."

CXXVIII.

The Love, which became stronger
in himself, after encountering Death
at the departure of Hallam,

"Is comrade to the lesser faith
That sees the course of human things."

This "lesser faith" attends to the
events of time, and is not overborne

by present confusions, but reaches, sustained by Love, to a last happy consummation.

If all that the "wild Hours" of Time had to do was to repeat the past, bring about useless wars, "fool the crowd with glorious lies," cleave religion into sects, disguise language, change governments, cramp learning, patch afresh what is antique and worn —if these results were all that could be effected, then would my scorn be well deserved. But

> " I see in part
> That all, as in some piece of art,
> Is toil co-operant to an end ; "

that all things are working together for final good.

CXXIX.

A more touching and tender address to the dead was never uttered than this Poem expresses, a more pure and

ennobling affection was never described. Sorrow is lost in the more
exalted sentiment of their certain
reunion, and in the strength derived
from a consciousness of the worthiness
of their past friendship.

> " Strange friend, past, present, and to be,
> Loved deeplier, darklier understood ;
> Behold, I dream a dream of good,
> And mingle all the world with thee."

CXXX.

Each had so participated in the
other's life : they had looked on
Nature with such kindred eyes,
having one mind and taste ; that
the survivor both sees and hears his
former companion in all objects and
sounds which present themselves.

Everything reminds him of Hallam ;
but

> " Tho' mix'd with God and Nature thou,
> I seem to love thee more and more."

His last declaration of devoted attachment is,

> "Far off thou art, but ever nigh;
>   I have thee still, and I rejoice;
>   I prosper, circled with thy voice;
> I shall not lose thee tho' I die."

CXXXI.

The concluding Poem is a direct address to the Deity. "O living will," surviving and enduring

> "When all that seems shall suffer shock"—

when the fashion of this world shall have passed away—

> "Rise in the spiritual rock"—

in our hearts, the one mediatorial channel, and flowing through our deeds, "make them pure." So that from "out of dust" we may cry, and be heard by One who has conquered Time and "with us works."

Thus we may be brought to an entire trust, and believe,

> " With faith that comes of self-control,
>   The truths that never can be proved
>   Until we close with all we loved,
> And all we flow from, soul in soul."

We emanate from the Deity : God breathed into man's nostrils, and he became a living soul. Our final destiny is, that God shall be " all in all : " not that all the souls of mankind shall be absorbed into the " general Soul," a notion which Poem xlvii. utterly repudiates ; but that the Divine nature shall be infused into and prevail in all.

PREFATORY POEM.

To this final confession of faith, worked out through Sorrow by the sustaining help of Love, the prefatory Poem is merely a pendent.

> " Strong Son of God, immortal Love,"

is addressed to Christ, God Himself upon earth. George Herbert had before called our Saviour

> " Immortal Love, author of this great frame ; "

and our Poet says, though we have not seen His face, we embrace Him by faith,

> " Believing where we cannot prove."

He acknowledges Him as the great Creator, and through all surrounding mysteries and disappointments, is satisfied with this conclusion as to the future,

> " Thou art just."

This conviction is enough.

> " Thou seemest human and divine,
>   The highest, holiest manhood, thou "—

God incarnate, to whom we must become spiritually united,

"Our wills are ours, to make them Thine,"

as expressed in Poem cxxxi., stanza 1.

"Our little systems" "are but broken lights of thee," even as the colours of the rainbow are the broken lights of the sun.

"We have but faith : we cannot know ;
For knowledge is of things we see."

Faith apprehends things which are spiritual, and do not come within the range of our senses ; whilst knowledge accepts only what can be seen and understood.

Hence, the Poet would have knowledge advance and increase to the utmost, "a beam in darkness" ever growing. But reverence must grow with it ; so that mind which accumulates knowledge, and soul which is the dwelling-place of faith, according well with each other, may make one music

—be in harmony "as before," that is, as in olden time; but now "vaster" in their compass, owing to greater reach of thought and research.

This warning against scientific assumptions, in opposition to spiritual truths, is repeated from Poem cxiv.

The concluding humble prayer, contained in the three last stanzas, has the true ring of devout piety.

> " Forgive what seem'd my sin in me ;
>   What seem'd my worth since I began ;
>   For merit lives from man to man,
> And not from man, O Lord, to Thee.
>
> " Forgive my grief for one removed,
>   Thy creature, whom I found so fair.
>   I trust he lives in Thee, and there
> I find him worthier to be loved.
>
> " Forgive these wild and wandering cries,
>   Confusions of a wasted youth ;
>   Forgive them where they fail in truth,
> And in thy wisdom make me wise."

SUPPLEMENTARY POEM.

The Epithalamium, or marriage lay, which is added to the great Poem, refers to the wedding of a younger sister, Cecilia Tennyson, who, about the year 1842, married Edmund Law Lushington, sometime professor of Greek at the University of Glasgow. I remember him as a boy at the Charterhouse, where, though so young as to be still in a short jacket, he was captain of the school when there were 450 scholars.

The strong domestic affections of the Poet are prominently shown throughout *In Memoriam*, and his pleasure at this bridal is very charming. He just recalls that Hallam had appreciated the Bride in her childhood :

> " O when her life was yet in bud,
> He too foretold the perfect rose."

The worth of the Bridegroom is acknowledged in this address :

> " And thou art worthy ; full of power ;
>   As gentle ; liberal-minded, great,
>   Consistent ; wearing all that weight
> Of learning lightly like a flower."

The whole Poem is pleasant and jocund, but scarcely harmonizes with the lofty solemnity of *In Memoriam*, whose author may rejoice in the thought, that he will leave behind him a rich legacy of comfort to all future generations of mourners.